SIT LIKE A BUDDHA

SIT LIKE A BUDDHA

A Pocket Guide to Meditation

Lodro Rinzler

Shambhala
Boston & London
2014

Shambhala Publications, Inc.
Horticultural Hall
300 Massachusetts Avenue
Boston, Massachusetts 02115
www.shambhala.com

9 8 7 6 5 4 3

Printed in the United States of America

⊗This edition is printed on acid-free paper that meets the
American National Standards Institute Z39.48 Standard.
♻This book is printed on 30% postconsumer recycled paper.
For more information please visit www.shambhala.com.

Distributed in the United States by Penguin Random House LLC
and in Canada by Random House of Canada Ltd

Library of Congress Cataloging-in-Publication Data

Rinzler, Lodro, author.
Sit like a Buddha: a pocket guide to meditation/Lodro Rinzler.—
First edition.
pages   cm
ISBN 978-1-61180-165-1 (alk. paper)
1. Meditation—Buddhism. I. Title.
BQ5612.R58 2014
294.3′4435—dc23
2014004049

For Milo, who is small. May this be of benefit when you are bigger.

CONTENTS

INTRODUCTION

I was raised Buddhist. I started practicing Buddhism at an early age. I began teaching it at the age of eighteen. But it is not Buddhism that has made me who I am. It is meditation. Meditation practice has calmed me when I felt anxious, softened me when I put up walls around my open heart, and allowed me to be more present in both the pleasurable and painful aspects of my life. I owe whatever contentment I have found in this life to meditation practice. That being said, I am honored to offer you this book, which will help you get a meditation practice going.

When I was eighteen years old I enrolled as a freshman at Wesleyan University and quickly began looking for a community to meditate with. I put posters up everywhere and a good number of people showed up for that first meeting. The only issue?

None of them knew how to meditate. There weren't a lot of available resources for meditation practice on my college campus; when I discussed this issue with a mentor he pointed out that I had attended a number of retreats that were prerequisites for a meditation instructor's training. "Why don't you do it?" he said. A few months later I was trained up and stumbling through offering meditation to others for the first time.

I would like to think that in the dozen-plus years I have been offering meditation instruction I have gotten better at it. Even if the words I say when I offer instruction have not shifted dramatically my understanding of them may have. Particularly when my first book, *The Buddha Walks into a Bar*, came out I found myself traveling a great deal and offering meditation to new practitioners in across North America. Meeting with thousands of individuals in the last few years has softened me, and allowed me to refine what it is we talk about when we talk about meditation.

I have never sat down and attempted to write a full book solely about meditation practice. Even though I've verbally presented these teachings before, I worry that the experience of meditation and how it has affected my life may lose its meaning in translation to these pages. I hope this volume is helpful, that it does aid you in establishing a meditation practice. If not (and even if it does) let me know. Getting a meditation practice going is a long journey, and I'm here to support you however I can. I'm easily found by e-mail, on Facebook, and on Twitter, and I post meditation videos regularly on YouTube.

I've had a firmly established meditation practice for a while and it has changed me in the most miraculous ways. It continues to allow me to be more present and compassionate as time goes on. If you follow along with this book, I believe you will establish a meditation practice, too, and will see the results of this transformative experience. This is a bit of an experiment, as this read does rely on your actually doing the practice introduced in these pages. Give meditation a chance and join me in this experiment, okay? To reiterate: I'm here for you; we'll do it together.

Lodro Rinzler
June 6, 2013
Brooklyn, New York

SIT LIKE A BUDDHA

STEP 1 / KNOW YOUR "WHY"

Whenever someone tells me that they are interested in meditating I always ask them why. They sometimes are surprised, thinking I would simply be overjoyed to learn that they are even remotely interested. Often I am and am just displaying an awesome poker face. However, I've found that if someone is not clear about why they want to meditate, they will soon find out that meditation is not necessarily easy and end up discouraged early on, not pursuing it in depth.

Similarly, when I offer meditation instruction through classes or at open houses at meditation centers I always begin with this question. "Why do you want to meditate?" I was in Washington, D.C., last year and was delighted yet surprised to see how many people came out on a Thursday night to hear me speak. "What is your motivation for coming here, to a meditation center, on a Thursday night?" I asked. "To quote Jay-Z, you could be anywhere in the world right now but you're here with me. There's a great *Parks and Rec* episode on TV tonight. Anyone want to share about their intention?" A gentleman raised his hand. He must have been in his mid-twenties. Someone handed him a microphone. "Well . . ." he said, "meditation seems cool so I thought I'd give it a try. Plus I own a DVR so I don't actually have to miss *Parks and Rec*."

I mention this story because there's a piece of good news behind it: in my experience in asking people why they are interested in checking out meditation there is never a wrong answer. Even if it's "I'm going to postpone my Thursday-night TV routine for an hour because I'm curious."

Granted, that answer is pretty rare. More often than not I hear that people want to be less stressed out, live more in the moment, or work more fluidly with their emotions. The other good news is that meditation helps with all of that. You just have to stick with it. To aid you in sticking with it, I've laid out ten steps that, if followed semiregularly, will get you a firmly formed meditation practice that you can do at home. By the end of this book not only will you feel confident in knowing how to meditate but, ideally, meditation will be a part of your everyday life.

Step 1 is about knowing your why, your intention. We'll return to that in a minute. Step 2 is learning a meditation technique. Step 3 is cultivating two tools needed for a strong meditation practice: mindfulness and awareness. Step 4 is learning to be consistent. Step 5 is developing a deep understanding of gentleness. Step 6 is discovering how to work with obstacles that come up in meditation. Step 7 is learning to move away from getting hooked by your emotions. Step 8 is connecting with your inherent peaceful state. Step 9 is becoming a dharmic, or authentic, practitioner. The final step, Step 10, is learning to rest in the present moment even when you're not on the meditation seat.

I truly believe that if you follow these ten steps not only will you have begun a meditation practice but you will have seen how it affects you in very positive ways. To begin with, though, we can't avoid that pesky question of "Why start to begin with?"

Exercise for Getting to "Why"

We'll get into the formal meditation posture in the next chapter but for now let's warm up by sitting up straight and taking a minute to check in with your body. Do a quick body scan, starting with your feet and working your way up to your skull. If you notice that you're particularly tense anywhere, bring a sense of relaxation to that spot. Once you feel a bit grounded, take a few deep breaths. Relax.

Now bring your full attention to this simple question: "What is my motivation for wanting to meditate?" Simply notice what answers arise in response to this question. The purpose of this contemplation is not to zero in on one answer and determine if it's logical. Allow whatever answers arise to swim across your mind and either disappear or return. Your key task is to just keep coming back to the question. If you get distracted and start thinking about what you want to have for lunch don't beat yourself up; just repeat the question to yourself: "What is my motivation for wanting to meditate?"

See if you can hold your mind to this one question for three minutes. You can set a timer if you like. At the end of that period of time drop the phrase entirely and take a few more deep breaths. As you arise from your contemplation period I have to ask: did any of those answers strike you as genuine? Was there one that kept coming up over and over again? If so, do you now know your "why" to get you going on this path of meditation?

You Always Have an Intention

There's a reason I'm needling you with this particular question. It's because you already live a life with intention, even if you don't realize it. To clarify, there's a line I'll draw in the sand: there's a difference between a conscious and an unconscious intention. A conscious intention is when you are able to tune in to your life and exhibit enough self-awareness that you can articulate the logic around why you are doing any given thing. So if someone catches you spending a lot of time on Facebook and they ask you why you're doing that, you actually have an answer, as opposed to saying, "I don't know. I'm bored?" An unconscious intention is just that sort of response; it's when you let your whims and habitual patterns yank your attention from one activity to the next without giving it much thought.

Let's take a pretty common example of having a conscious versus an unconscious intention. You go out with friends on a Saturday night. You know you're going to drink and likely dance, maybe talk to members of the sex you're attracted to, maybe even make out or something. That's cool. Really. I'm all for it. Making out is fun. That is, assuming you consciously intend to do those things, after some level of reflection. That means you have a conscious intention to do whatever you're going to do on a Saturday night.

More often than not we go out with friends, launch into a new relationship, or jump ship from one job to another without a clear understanding of why we're doing those things. We never pause and develop a conscious intention and, as a result, things tend to get messy down the road.

To return to our example you could have had a rough week and you go out straight from work. You feel like there is no time to pause and reflect, and try to live with a conscious intention. So you drink too much to forget the jerks you work with, then because you drink too much you end up tripping over yourself while dancing, making a fool of yourself around people you want to make out with, and continue to drink to avoid dealing with any of these rough emotions of aggression and embarrassment. You then end up vomiting them out, alongside your gin and tonics, at the end of the night. Nice drink choice, by the way.

Let's step back and go through the same scenario but with a conscious intention. You leave work but you decide to take a respite first. You go for a walk, or sit in a park, or swing by home for a shower. You take some time and reflect on your day, allow for the transition from work to fun to happen, and then contemplate "What is my intention for tonight?" After a few minutes of returning to that question (even while you're grocery shopping or walking about) you realize that you just want to connect with the friends you're going to see because you don't get to see them enough. You head out and instead of getting wasted you enjoy a few drinks with them, relax together, and reconnect. Whether you dance or meet other people or not it's all okay because you're living in line with your conscious intention.

That is a long-winded answer to the question about why I'm needling you about finding your personal motivation for meditation practice. It's because I'm a firm believer that when you live your life in line with conscious intentions, as opposed to unconscious ones, you live a fuller, happier life overall. And throw up less.

THIS IS IMPORTANT

I'm not normally such a hard-ass right out of the gate in my books, but this is the foundational step in our journey together so I feel like we need to do it right. The reason this is so important is because meditation practice is hard. There. I said it. I admit it. It has a zillion benefits, ranging from health improvement to stress reduction to overall enjoyment of life, but it's a long journey and the markers of success are not always obvious. So when you feel disheartened (more on disheartenment in chapter 6) you can look back at this very basic foundation block and say, "Oh right. That's why I'm doing this. I want to be kinder / more self-aware / less stressed out all the time." Having that solid understanding of why you're doing this work (and let's be clear, it's work) will help you out long term.

In fact, if you now have your intention ready, write it down. We'll even give you some space at the bottom of this page. Jot it down. Only you have to know. Or if you want other people to know feel free to e-mail it to me and then let me know how it works out when you're done with the book. Your intention may shift a little or change dramatically over these next steps to establishing your meditation practice, but this is a great one to start with. So do you have your why? Good. Let's get into the action now.

My intention in beginning to meditate is_____

_____

_____

_____

STEP 2 / LEARN THE MEDITATION TECHNIQUE

The meditation practice we will be pursuing in this volume is called *shamatha*, or calm-abiding meditation. There are many different forms of meditation one could pursue, to different ends. Some meditation practices could help you fall asleep easier, for example. This one is the exact opposite of that, although it does have a calming effect. Shamatha is intended to wake you up.

If you want to be more present with your work, this is your practice. If you want to connect with friends and family in a genuine way, this is your practice. If you want to be there for both the pleasurable and painful elements throughout your life, this is your practice. Shamatha wakes you up to what is going on in this very moment, through training in paying attention to something that embodies this moment: the breath.

The breath is always fresh. It's always what is going on right now. We were born breathing and we will breathe until we die. It is always with us. Yet we don't think about it. We don't often spend time contemplating something as simple and natural as the breath. Until now.

This particular practice dates back to the time of the Buddha. The Buddha, before he was the Buddha, was a prince by the name of Siddhartha Gautama. He was raised in a very sheltered existence and did not see suffering throughout his childhood and teenage years. Finally he became curious about what occurred beyond the walls of his palace so, with his father's blessing, he went on a carriage ride. As he encountered the outside world, despite his father's wishes, he got his first glimpse of suffering: he saw old age, sickness, and death. He also saw an ascetic, and, feeling overwhelmed by the realization of suffering, he decided to choose that spiritual career path instead of the kingly one.

Siddhartha snuck out from his father's home and spent his twenties and into his thirties exploring various spiritual practices, learning a wide variety of meditation techniques that sought to accomplish different things. He would master them quickly and then move on to find some new practice, as none of the ones he encountered alleviated that sense of suffering he had newly discovered.

Finally he sat down under a tree and decided, "Let me meditate on the breath for a bit." He did, and resolved to not get up until he attained enlightenment. All sorts of mental anguish arose but still he sat there. Ultimately he achieved his goal: he attained nirvana. Before it was a '90s grunge band, *nirvana* was a term reserved solely for achieving a state of peace. Often when people think of nirvana they think of someone sitting there blissed out. That's not what Siddhartha achieved.

When Siddhartha attained enlightenment, or nirvana, he became in tune with the way reality is. Not his idea of what reality should be, or some transcendent notion of what it could be, but he woke up to the way things are. That's enlightenment. That is why he became known as a buddha, or Awakened One.

In taking on this simple sitting practice that the Buddha did, you are taking on a commitment to wake up. You may not have the desire to achieve ultimate enlightenment, and that's fine, I promise, but the idea of being more awake and in tune with your life might sound appealing. With that aspiration in mind, let's review the specific instruction for shamatha meditation.

Begin by taking a comfortable seat on a cushion on the ground. If it will hurt to sit on the ground you can sit instead in a chair. In either situation, sit with your butt firmly in the center of your seat. You want to feel a sense of being grounded, physically, which will help ground you mentally. Feel the weight of your body on the earth. If you are on a cushion, loosely cross your legs with your knees falling a little bit below your hip bones. If you are in a chair, place your feet firmly on the ground about hip-width apart.

From this strong base you expand upward toward the sky. Elongate your spine in order to sit up straight. Don't throw your shoulders back or you will end up sore and in pain. Actually connect with your skeletal curvature and use that as the basis for your support. If visualizing is helpful I always recommend imagining a string at the top of your head, pulling you straight up. Many of us have spent decades slouching over as we sit reading, working at computers, and the like, so it's not uncommon that this may initially be uncomfortable or even a bit agonizing. I promise you that it gets easier over time. For now please exert yourself to stick with this upright posture. Do not lean back if you are in a chair.

Now drop your hands at your sides for a moment. Pick them up at the elbows and drop them, palms down, on your thighs. This specific positioning should allow for a bit of extra support for your back. In some traditions you may have seen people keep their palms face up or in a special mudra, or hand positioning, at the navel. Those positions are fine and good, but let's keep it simple and provide some additional posture support by keeping our palms face-down on our thighs.

Your skull rests at the top of your spine. The only thing you need to do positioning-wise there is to slightly tuck in your chin. Relax the muscles in your face, particularly in your forehead, around your eyes, and your jaw. That might mean that your jaw hangs open, which is preferred. You can place your tongue up against the roof of your mouth, which slows down the swallowing process and allows for clear breathing.

Finally, rest your gaze about two to four feet ahead of you on the ground. It may surprise you that I recommend keeping your eyes open. It's a matter of view. If you intend to become more awake to what is going on around you it seems counterproductive to close your eyes. I have found that for people who are brand-new to meditation, this is not so hard. For those who have meditated in the past with their eyes closed it is a bit of a struggle to make this transition. Still, I highly encourage you to try to keep your eyes open, letting your gaze fall ahead of you in a relaxed manner.

Meditation is not an intellectual exercise. It is about connecting with what is going on in your body. This process of connecting to your body, as it is, is extremely important. So take the time to properly connect with and drop into your physical being before moving on.

BREATH

Now for the hard part, which I realize sounds quite simple: bring your full attention to the breath. You are breathing while you read this book. You breathe all day. You even breathe when you sleep. It's not something you often pay attention to. But now do it. Even if you're not attempting meditation at this moment. Maybe you're on the subway. Or in a waiting room. Just put down the book and pay attention to your breath for one minute.

It's not so easy is it? Our mind is habituated to running amok, not staying focused on something as basic as the breath. This is why meditation practice is difficult. We have spent years habituating ourselves to do anything other than be present with what is going on in this very moment. The breath serves as our anchor to the present. So feel your breathing, as it is right now.

Please note that you don't need to alter or change your breath from its normal pattern. You don't need to emphasize either the out-breath or the in-breath. Just breathe like you normally do. You may even find yourself self-conscious about how you are breathing. Relax. Let your body naturally do its thing. In some sense, the true object of your meditation practice is appreciation of your very being.

MIND

You will get distracted from the breath. It may be a few seconds or it may be minutes but you will get distracted. That's also very natural. Since we are not used to being in the present moment the mind habitually gravitates toward the past and future. For instance, you may attempt to be present but you start reliving a conversation you had with someone who annoyed you earlier. From there your mind jumps to the future and how you will tell that person off the next time you see them.

In any such case where your attention gets stolen by the past or future just remember that your intention is to be present with the breath. If your mind is lost in big thoughts that take you out of the room you can silently and gently say "thinking" to yourself as a reminder that what you are doing is very normal but not what you want to do. Having labeled your discursive thought "thinking," you can bring your attention back to the breath again.

That is the very basic shamatha practice. It is what the Buddha did and it worked for him, so we really ought to give it a solid chance. We don't need extra practices or new techniques to challenge ourselves. For the course of our work together please use this shamatha practice. Its power is in its simplicity. Over time you will get to see yourself more clearly. You will become a connoisseur of your own thought process. That is what a meditator is; someone who appreciates the many flavors of their own mind and is able to be present with all of them. Next, let's look at two tools that will aid us in this endeavor.

STEP 3 / APPLY THE ULTIMATE
TAG-TEAM COMBO

Having dipped your toe in the waters of meditation you may realize this practice can be challenging. It's called calm-abiding meditation, but your mind feels like it has gone crazy. In fact, it's not uncommon for beginning meditators to feel as if they have opened the floodgates and there is a barrage of thoughts pummeling them, as if they were standing at the bottom of a waterfall and thoughts just hit them with that level of speed and velocity. It can feel that overwhelming.

The good news is (and trust me I speak from experience here) it gets easier. As you begin to meditate consistently you start to gradually see an increase in the ability to stay with the breath and be more present, both on the meditation cushion and with various elements of the rest of your life. It does take a little bit of time for that to happen, so best to explore the shamatha practice regularly as we go through these next steps.

At this point I want to introduce some meditative aids. These are two tools that will help us with our meditation practice: mindfulness and awareness. Slap them on your tool belt because they are, respectively, the drill and measuring tape of your practice. You will continuously use them throughout your time meditating, so it's best to become familiar with them early on.

First, let's define these things. The Tibetan word for mindfulness is *trenpa*, which, if we want to get long-winded about it, can also be translated as "the ability to hold your attention to something." That is pretty straightforward, right? If you want to be mindful of the breath that means you are holding your attention to your breathing. If you want to be mindful of a conversation it means fully engaging that discussion. If you want to be mindful while you eat it means paying attention to and enjoying your meal. Mindfulness is the simple act of being fully with whatever you are doing. "Ness" in this sense implies the essence of, so when we say "mindfulness" we are saying we are cultivating the essence of being mindful, or being present.

Mindfulness is an inherent capacity that we all have. It's not something we need to go out and buy at the supermarket. We already possess it. This tool, this drill, is already on our tool belt. We just need to learn how to use it. I use the example of the drill because mindfulness is a precise instrument; it specifically keeps us attuned to the present moment. While it may feel uncomfortable or difficult to be mindful with the breath, it is in fact just applying this tool to retrain our mind to do something it's very accustomed to doing in other ways.

What I mean is that we are actually always meditating on something. We could be meditating on that hottie we saw earlier today and wondering what it would be like to go out with him or her, where we would take them, and whether we would kiss them (or more) at the end of the night. Or we could be meditating on an upcoming work project and all the people we need to meet with, going so far as to make mental drafts of the e-mails we need to send. The point here is that our mind is always being placed on something. More often than not our mind is being placed on something other than what is going on right now. Our mind is accustomed to meditating on the future and the past, but we need to retrain it to come back to the present. That is the power of mindfulness: we learn to be precise with the breath as an anchor to the present so that later on we are more mindful with the rest of our lives.

The second tool I want to mention at this point is

our trusty measuring tape of awareness. The Tibetan word for awareness is *sheshin*. *She* can be translated into English as "knowing," while *shin* is "present." In other words, we can think of this phrase as "presently knowing," or knowing what is going on in this very moment. It is a sense of awareness of our environment, both our physical environment and our mental environment. This tool of awareness is, not unlike mindfulness, something we already possess.

Mindfulness and awareness work together to keep us engaged in the present moment. They are the tag team of meditative tools. In the case of our physical environment, we may be going about our day and we hear our phone ring. In this example, it is awareness that says, "Oh. Hey. My phone is ringing." Recognizing that a noise occurred and that it is your telephone is an awareness of your physical environment. Then you pick up your phone and begin talking to whomever called you, and become fully engaged in that conversation. That is mindfulness bringing you to the point where you are truly in the moment with a dialogue. Maybe the person on the other end of the phone starts to bore you at some point and you lose your sense of mindfulness. When they call you on that and say, "Are you even listening to me?" your awareness will snap you back to what is going on in the moment and you will once more be present with that person.

Another example could be where you are waiting in line at a coffee shop. You might be very distracted at first, looking at your e-mail on your phone, or spacing out, but then the barista says "next" and there you are, fully present with that person, explaining your order, trying to engage in polite chitchat, and having a genuine human interaction. Awareness is what registers the barista calling "next" and mindfulness is what keeps you present enough to order your coffee. Minutes later someone calls out your name. Awareness picks up that your name has been called and mindfulness, ideally, comes into play while you sit down to taste and enjoy your drink.

In the case of our mental environment, awareness is that aspect of our mind that notices when we are no longer present with the breath. You know how you can be sitting there meditating, then all of a sudden a few minutes have passed and you have been plotting out that vacation you may or may not ever take, and then you catch yourself and say, "Whoa! Get back to meditating on the breath"? Awareness is that little voice guiding you back to your meditation practice. I am referring to it as the measuring tape because it can judge how very far you have gone from the present moment and then snap you back to the breath, like the tape snapping back into its base. Another way to think of awareness is that it is the sheriff of the small town of your mind, constantly and kindly keeping watch and enforcing your ability to come back to your breathing.

My teacher Sakyong Mipham Rinpoche has said, "Every moment has its energy; either it will ride us, or we can ride it."[1] If we do not live our lives with mindfulness and awareness we are missing a lot of opportunities to enjoy all the little moments throughout our day. We are instead letting our habitual patterns play out randomly as the energy of the moment rides us. It is a bit like listening to some horribly indulgent elevator music on a never-ending ride where every stop along the way opens the doors to self-involvement and suffering. If you are able to be in the moment and recognize the energy of what is going on, you can live your life with intention. If you cannot ride the energy of this very moment then it will ride you; in other words you will live a life based in unconscious intentions, held hostage to whatever discursive whims your mind cooks up. No matter what floor of the elevator you get off at it will lead to pain and inner turmoil.

If you apply these two tools of mindfulness and awareness to your meditation practice it will flourish. These two natural weapons of our practice will guide us back to that feeling of calm that is advertised in the title of our calm-abiding meditation. Your awareness will pop up when you get distracted and, like that tape measure rolling in on itself, snap you back to the present moment. It will say "thinking." Then we return to mindfulness of the breath. When we catch ourselves and say "thinking," it's like a trick where we hit that elevator button that allows us to get off into a spacious, cool environment where we can enjoy our lives.

You may get lost in thought again but awareness, the loyal friend that it is, will once more catch you: "thinking." Then you return to applying mindfulness to the physical sensation of both your inbreath and your out-breath. It goes on like that until these two tools become second nature and you are resting more and more with the breath and with your life.

Another word for meditation in Tibetan is *gom.* It can also be translated as "become familiar with." In the process of meditation we are essentially becoming more familiar with our own mind and our habitual patterns. Now that you are beginning to look at your mind you can treat it like a new acquaintance. You may at first view that waterfall of thoughts that occurs when you sit down to meditate and say, "Um . . . I don't know if I want to get to know you, Mr. Mind," but you persevere and as you continue to apply mindfulness and awareness you become more accustomed to the eccentricities of your own mental being. Just like when you make a new friend, you start to appreciate their peculiarities. In this way, meditation is essentially a process of becoming friends with yourself.

A senior teacher in the Shambhala tradition, Pema Chödrön, has said, "In practicing meditation, we're not trying to live up to some kind of ideal—quite the opposite. We're just being with our experience, whatever it is."[2] Your mind may sometimes be chaotic; it may sometimes be peaceful. In either case, if you can investigate it through simply being present then you are becoming more thoroughly who you are. You are more able to be with your experience, whether it is good or bad.

As a bonus, when you continue to apply mindfulness and awareness while meditating you will find that they will naturally manifest more as you go about your day-to-day life. You will end up being more present with friends when you go out to dinner, or lovers when you are in bed, or family members even if you are in an argument. In all of these situations you can tune in to the present moment. You can be mindful of what is going on right now. You can maintain awareness of your environment and who you are relating to. With the tag-team combination of the precise drill of mindfulness and the rapid-fire snap of the measuring tape of awareness you can live a fuller, more content life overall, in tune with the way things are.

STEP 4 / BE CONSISTENT

Having set upon an intention for beginning a meditation practice, learned the basic technique of how to do it, and discovered the important tools of mindfulness and awareness, you are ready to establish a regular meditation practice at home. The name of the game for this step of the path is "consistency." If you want to get a meditation practice going, you will need a consistent environment, scheduled time, amount of time, and pacing to make sure it's feasible for you. If you can master these four things then your meditation practice will gradually integrate into your life and have a profound effect on you. In this chapter I'll lay out all the discipline aspects of what it takes to really get going, but in the next chapter we'll temper the hardcore discipline with the following step, which is learning to be truly gentle with yourself.

Imagine getting home at night after a long day of work and you're exhausted. Here's the thing though: you don't have a consistent space to sleep so you have to assemble your bed. You get the frame set up, screw it together, insert the flats, lay the mattress on top, and then put on the sheets and pillows. Sounds like a lot of work for something you're going to do every day, right?

That's what it's like for many people in terms of creating an environment for their meditation practice. More often than not new people will grab the cushions off the couch, move the TV out of the corner, throw the cushions down, plop down on them, and expect to have a really great meditation session. In other words, they make getting to the meditation cushion itself harder than it has to be.

Imagine instead that you wake up in the morning and roll out of bed and there's a little corner in your living room that's already set up to meditate. It's inviting you to practice, right off the bat. All you have to do is sit down for a bit and enjoy your meditation. That sounds better, right? That's the beauty of having a consistent environment for your meditation practice.

As Sakyong Mipham Rinpoche has said, "The environment is a support or a deterrent for whatever we want to do. Everything in our environment—food, clothing, places, the hours we keep, the compassion or jealousy of others—affects us."[1] If you want to establish a meditation practice at home, one of the most important things you can do is create a supportive environment for yourself. Take a moment today to look at your home. Based on what it currently looks like, you can ask yourself, "What is my environment supporting?" Are there clothes strewn about, piles of dishes in the sink, and knick-knacks everywhere? If so, that likely serves as a deterrent for cultivating qualities of awakeness or peace. If your environment is clean, with art that inspires you hung here and there, and everything you own in its proper place, that will more likely support those qualities.

Living in New York, I am used to working with people who do not have a lot of room to spare to establish a meditation environment. If you live in a home and have been wondering what to do with your spare bedroom, a meditation room might be in order. But if you live in a small apartment then you may find that you only have a corner of your living room or bedroom to spare for a meditation space. In either case, you can set up a consistent meditation environment.

I do recommend getting a meditation cushion if you are serious about getting a regular practice going. You can buy one locally or order one online (see the Resources section for more information). Having a cushion sitting out in the open is an easy way to set an expectation for where you go to meditate. All you have to do is sit down and you're ready to start. Often they are brightly colored, so as you go about your day it is always there to catch your eye and remind you that you intend to meditate at some point.

There are a few types of cushions one could choose from, ranging from the *zafu*, a circular cushion that is a bit low to the ground, to the *gomden*, which is a rectangular cushion that has the look of a cushion but the firm seat of a chair. A wide variety of meditation benches are also available out there. If you live near a meditation center you can try these cushions out and see what feels right to you.

At the same time, I realize not everyone wants to invest in a meditation cushion right off the bat. You could use pillows from your bed, or couch cushions, or anything else that gives you a bit of a lift up off the ground and allows you to sit in the meditation posture comfortably. Or you can sit in a chair with four legs (ones with wheels will be distracting) and place your feet hips-width apart solidly on the ground.

If you are bringing a chair, pillows, or cushions

from other areas of your home you can establish a regular meditation space in other ways. You could place a Buddha statue on a small stool in your meditation corner and that will serve as a similar reminder to go to that space and meditate. Or you can have a candle that attracts you and you can light it for the duration of your meditation sessions. Or you can purchase an incense burner that you feel is uplifting and dignified. In any of these situations the important thing is that the space is consistent and magnetizing to you. That way you don't have to work too hard to get your daily practice going.

CONSISTENT TIMING

In addition to having a consistent environment, it's important to identify a consistent time of day that you are able to meditate. There's a fine line you have to walk in figuring out when you want to meditate; you want to be awake but not in the midst of a chaotic schedule. For some people that means they wake up in the morning and sit right down in their meditation environment. For others that means they have their morning shower or coffee and then practice. Some people never find the time to meditate in the morning and prefer to do it right when they get home from school or work. Others do it during their lunch break. Some lucky people are even able to meditate right before bed and don't fall asleep during their session!

It actually took me years to figure out the best time of day for me to meditate. At this point I get up, shower, check in on my workload, engage it for a half hour, and then force myself to close the laptop and sit down on the cushion. In my case I am awake enough so I'm not sitting there feeling groggy but my mind hasn't sped up to full "have to get all my work done" mode yet.

The thing I have found is that if I set an exact time for my meditation practice I may end up frustrated when I get delayed. For example, if I said that I'm going to meditate every day at 8:45 a.m. and yet my dog takes longer than I expected while I'm walking her, I might sit down and meditate on how late my dog always makes me. That's not very helpful. Instead, I have learned that it's best to just acknowledge my usual schedule and insert meditation in just like I would other aspects of my morning routine. In that way I'm not too rigid but it still holds a place of importance in my day. As you begin to meditate consistently, look over your weekly schedule and see if there is a time of day you can meditate regularly. Making a conscious choice in this regard is helpful so that you don't keep switching it up helter-skelter, ultimately convincing yourself that on a given day you didn't have the time to squeeze it in.

CONSISTENT AMOUNT OF TIME

Another form of consistency that is helpful for newer practitioners is picking an amount of time for practice and sticking to it. I generally recommend starting with ten minutes a day. We all have ten minutes a day. Even if you're super-busy and your kids demand a lot of your attention and your boss is a jerk and calls you at home all the time, you still can sneak ten minutes a day in the morning or evening. Finding those ten minutes will be the tricky thing but sticking to that ten shouldn't be too hard.

One thing I would caution against is sitting down with the intention of sitting for one period of time but midway through changing your mind. Sometimes you might sit down to meditate and ten minutes will feel like forever. You will worry that your timer is broken and glance at your clock and see it's only been three minutes and you will want to leap off the meditation seat. Don't do that. Sit for those ten minutes. The next day you may be staying with your breath and the timer will go off and you'll think, "Maybe I have time for another ten." Don't do that either.

When you start to go down that road of adjusting the amount of time you're meditating while in the act of meditation (a) you're using your meditation as a source of distracting yourself from your meditation and (b) you're starting to judge your meditation practice. Don't ever judge your meditation practice. Your mind is your mind. Sometimes it will be easy to stay with the breath and you'll think you're an inch from enlightenment. The next day someone at work pisses you off and that's all you can think about when you sit down to meditate. We should never label our practice sessions as "good" or "bad." Any time you get to the meditation seat is good meditation. That is why it is important to stick with a consistent amount of time you are meditating. If, over time, you want to increase that amount another five or ten minutes do so, but do so consistently.

CONSISTENT PACING

A number of studies have come out lately about how long it takes for people to form habits. I recently read that if you want to construct a new habit you should do the same thing eleven days in a row and your brain starts to register it as something that you regularly do. My understanding is that this could be eleven days without smoking, or eleven days of writing a little bit, and these new things you are doing start to become habit-forming. After twenty-one days the habit is set.

I began meditating when I was quite young, attending weekend retreats at the age of eleven. However, it was only when I was seventeen that I began a daily meditation practice. It was a direct result of attending a month-long meditation retreat in Nova Scotia at a small monastery known as Gampo Abbey. It was a truly transformative experience for me and as I left the monastery I swore to myself that I would keep meditating regularly. Somehow, it was easier than I thought. Only years later do I realize that the level of consistency that was offered as I began to pace myself in establishing a practice was a direct result of that retreat. Yes, it was a powerful experience to be away from everything, but the fact that I meditated every day for more than twenty-one days worked the meditation practice into my bones to the point where it became second nature. Going home after that it was easier to stick with the practice.

That being said, I can't emphasize enough the importance of pacing yourself and meditating consistently, day after day, as you get your meditation practice off the ground (figuratively; you likely will not be levitating). If you can, set aside eleven days in a row that will launch your regular meditation practice. See if it starts to be more habitual after that initial period. If you're doing ten minutes a day, that is 110 minutes—less than two hours—of your life that will set you up for a lifetime of being more present, kinder, and more compassionate. As far as investments of time go, that's a pretty sweet deal.

At times you will find that one of these elements is hard to achieve. For example, you may travel and find it impossible to have a consistent environment within which you can meditate. In that situation, I always recommend taking an element of your home setup on the road with you. For me, I often travel with a statue of the Buddhist being Manjushri, known to embody wisdom. It was a gift from a friend and holds personal significance to me, so whether I am staying with friends or in a hotel I know that if I set it out I will be attracted to it and be reminded to meditate. For you it might be a photo of a role model you would like to emulate as a result of your practice or a memento from a spiritual journey you took. Whatever it may be, bring it with you on the road and allow it to inspire you to meditate.

The more you are able to keep consistent with your practice the more it will become natural to your life and who you are. I recommend that you maintain a consistent environment to support your meditation practice, stick to a consistent time of day that you know works for you to meditate, keep a consistent amount of time that feels workable for you to sit, and launch your practice with consistent pacing. If you can do these four things you will be that much closer to integrating this transformative practice into your day-to-day being. Now that we've covered those various forms of discipline, let's take a look at the next step on our journey: learning to be gentle.

STEP 5 / BE GENTLE

Growing up I read a lot of comic books. In fact, I still sometimes read them. Actually, I read them a fair amount. There is something about comic-book superheroes who, whether it's through scientific accident or being born differently, acquire certain skills and, most importantly, decide to do some good with them that I've found endearing and inspiring. The older I get, though, the less fantasy-based these superheroes seem. I have had the opportunity to meet many extraordinary people who have survived harrowing adventures and benefited the world greatly, without having the advantage of wielding superhuman powers. These are real-life superheroes to me, and as a result of their influence I've decided to make up a superhero: Gentleness Man.

Gentleness Man was born one day when he realized he didn't have to be such a jerk to himself. That's his origin story. In that moment realization dawned and since then he has spent his life learning to master his habitual desire to act out in harmful ways. He sees aggression in himself and others and counters it with (surprise surprise) gentleness. His unique power is that he can offer kindness in all situations. Here's the reveal: you could be this superhero.

You can be Gentleness Man or Gentleness Woman. If you have ever said, "I really ought to be kinder to myself," you have already had your origin story. Your superheroic path is to deepen your conviction in that realization and have the follow-through to actually be gentle. You know there are times when you're a jerk to yourself and act out in ways that hurt others. You can choose not to do that. You can dedicate your life to being the very embodiment of gentleness.

There is an obstacle here, which is your archnemesis, Self-Aggression. Self-Aggression manifests in a thousand different ways every week, but each time, as Gentleness Woman or Gentleness Man, you can sidestep Self-Aggression's plan through being mindful and self-aware. By utilizing those tools of mindfulness and awareness discussed in the previous chapter you can learn to not give in to aggressive thinking and remain present.

Here is an example of one of Self-Aggression's

nefarious plots: as you sit down to meditate you may find yourself frustrated that you can't simply be with what is going on in your body. You have trouble finding the breath, and when you do you immediately get distracted and get taken for a ride by a big thought. You ignore awareness and continue riding that fantasy or emotion. Eventually you start to acknowledge that you're not being present and say "thinking" to yourself repeatedly. Then the way you're saying "thinking" in your head gets louder. You're not being mindful and that's annoying you. Eventually you're yelling *thinking!* over and over again at yourself and wondering why you're not finding inner peace. That's when Self-Aggression wins the day.

He doesn't have to. In that moment when you catch yourself not being mindful or aware, you don't have to beat yourself up about it. You can instead just say "thinking" very gently to yourself, and come back to the breath. You don't have to judge yourself for losing track of the breath. You don't have to get frustrated. When you see those reactions arise just remind yourself that gentleness is the better option and relax into that state. When you are able to return to gentleness you will find that such an option brings you back to the breath a thousand times better than self-aggression ever would.

Let's instead look at one way that Gentleness

Man or Gentleness Woman would counter this plot. To begin, our hero would take the time to express gentleness to himself before he even sat down to practice. He knows that his mind has been running loose all day, bouncing from one activity to another, engaging work, family, his relationship, everything. His mind is pretty wild so instead of going straight to meditate he offers himself gentleness by easing into the practice. He drinks a cup of tea or water and allows his mind to begin to shift from a lot of activity to simply tasting his beverage. Then he stretches a bit, to bring him more into his body. When he sits down he reads a few pages of his favorite Buddhist book, thus taking in some of the teachings around what he is about to do. Each of these activities is a small gesture of kindness to him, laying the ground for a gentle period of meditation.

As a result of these simple offerings to himself he finds that he is more able to simply be with what is going on in his body. He may have a bit of trouble staying with the breath but he reminds himself that this is natural, and he is patient, gently checking in with his posture and breath again. Then a big thought arises: he forgot to e-mail his boss some important information. Instead of beating himself up or mentally yelling *"thinking!"* he offers himself a moment of forgiveness and relaxes back into being with the breath. He spends his ten minutes learning more about himself while reinforcing the habit of being gentle.

When you are gentle with yourself on the meditation cushion you find that you are getting better at staying with the breath relatively quickly. You enjoy your meditation time more because it's not a time where you continue the exhausting parade of self-criticism. You are relaxing into what is going on in the moment, which feels kind and gentle. That gentleness then extends beyond your time on the meditation seat. Sakyong Mipham Rinpoche has said, "What are the signs of progress? Our body, speech, and mind become more gentle."[1] Through being gentle and bringing a sense of relaxing with the breath to your practice, you start to see that your body becomes more gentle in how you move through the world, your speech is kinder and more pleasant when you engage others, and your mind embodies this basic quality.

I call the quality of gentleness basic because, from a Buddhist perspective, it is innate to who we are. I will discuss the concept of peaceful abiding and what we discover when we do quiet our mind in chapter 8, but as a preview I want to hark back to the time of the Buddha once more. When the Buddha attained enlightenment he saw things as they are. He saw that Self-Aggression was self-enforced. It is learned behavior, not a part of our inherent state. Similarly fear, ignorance, pride, and many more harmful states that we perpetuate are not innate to who we are. They are things we pick up along the way. The core of who we are, according to the Buddha's experience, is awake. It is good. That means we are innately wise, worthy, strong, and (believe it or not) gentle beings. That is our birthright. The meditation practice is simply discovering that for yourself, cultivating those qualities, and acting from them.

If you don't believe me that's okay. Trust your experience. In my experience this has turned out to be true. In fact, I was sitting with my godson today and he reified this notion for me. Milo is two and a half years old. However, in spending time with him, I have never seen him fall victim to Self-Aggression. He doesn't know that he should be working more hours or calling his mother more. Why would he? He hasn't been exposed to too many societal expectations. For now, he is simply gentle to himself. Through being very gentle to himself he has learned to be gentle to others. He is a very kind being. I am guessing that at some point someone will tell him he has done something very wrong and that realization will stay with him so that he starts to beat himself up about it. But for now he embodies gentleness. That shows me, for what may be the millionth time, that we are born with this quality.

One way I have seen Self-Aggression rear its head is through something I call "Buddhist guilt." It's not unlike thinking you should be working more or calling your mother more. In fact, it's not unlike what is commonly referred to as Jewish guilt. It's the notion that you ought to be spending more time meditating. It's that sinking feeling when you commit to meditating eleven days in a row like I suggested in the previous chapter but then on day 5 something comes up and you skip your practice session and feel like an asshole about it. That's a moment when Self-Aggression can jump out of the bushes and really clobber you. "You said you were going to be a meditator. You couldn't even last five days!"

As Gentleness Woman (or Man) you need to fight against this particular version of Self-Aggression. When you experience Buddhist guilt over not meditating enough or not meditating consistently the trick is to just give yourself a break. In general when you feel like you're tightening up and taking your meditation practice too seriously this is my advice. Just apply gentleness through the give-yourself-a-break method. This method involves dropping that judgmental voice in your head and instead acknowledging that this is a difficult practice and you will, assuming you live a nice long life, have many more days within which you can practice. Apply gentleness in all of these areas of your life and you will find that your practice becomes easier, more enjoyable, and that gentleness begins to infiltrate your body, speech, and mind even when you're not actually meditating. Thus you are already seeing the fruits of your meditative labor. Congratulations!

STEP 6 / OVERCOME THE THREE MAIN OBSTACLES

To kick a dead horse: meditation is tough. I feel like I need to keep reminding you of that though, or you might become discouraged. It isn't just tough for you; it's tough for everyone. That is why I mention cultivating the quality of gentleness early on in this process. That is a foundational aspect of what we need to cultivate in order to progress along the path. In particular, gentleness remains important as we start to face habitual obstacles to our practice.

Within a traditional framework there are three main obstacles we can reflect on. Think of these as somewhat large umbrellas under which we group anything that comes up that distracts you from maintaining a regular meditation practice. These three obstacles are: laziness, speedy-busyness, and disheartenment. You may have already started to meditate regularly and encountered these obstacles in some form. Or you may sit down tomorrow and experience them for the first time. In either case, they will arise, so it is best to know them well and know how to overcome them.

LAZINESS

Laziness from a meditation point of view often shows up as feeling an aversion to the practice itself. It often takes the form of convincing yourself you don't have to do it. It can be as simple as waking up in the morning, hearing the rain hitting your window, feeling the warmth of your comforter, and looking over at the meditation cushion in the corner of your room with disdain. That meditation cushion isn't nearly as warm and cozy as your bed, and you deserve an extra twenty minutes of sleep, so you figure you ought to just skip your meditation practice. That's laziness.

Or perhaps when you sit down to meditate you sit there and space out. You forget to apply the meditation technique of being with the breath, or you start that but as soon as a hot fantasy arises it seems easier to play around with that than apply the technique of once again returning to the breath. Sometimes when you sit down it's an enjoyable experience. Other times it can be a pain in the neck to stay with the meditation instruction. Both occur for everyone and, as a result, it's not unusual to feel a bit of aversion or laziness as a habitual way to worm out of it.

If you find yourself struggling to get to your meditation seat, just remember to take it easy on yourself, drop judgment, and exert yourself just a little more than you are comfortable with. Note that the first part of that advice addresses whatever Self-Aggression throws at you. You may feel the warm comfort of your bed, start to justify that it's okay to skip a day of practice, and then immediately loathe yourself for thinking that. That moment is when you remember to give yourself a break and drop judgment.

The second part of this advice involves swinging your feet over the edge of the bed and hopping down. Exert yourself this small amount beyond your comfort level and you will find that you feel good about it. It is the same principle as lifting a little bit more than what you might normally at the gym or running a bit faster or farther than you have before; this level of exertion is counter to maintaining our comfort level but feels so good once you've engaged it. This same advice goes for when you do make it to the meditation seat and feel a tendency arise to space out or ignore the instructions. Come back to the breath, over and over again. Apply yourself and you will enjoy your practice more.

SPEEDY-BUSYNESS

Counter to what we normally perceive as laziness is our second main obstacle: speedy-busyness. I first heard this term used by my teacher, Sakyong Mipham Rinpoche, and it seems to hit the nail on the head. It's the idea that you know you want to meditate. It's definitely something you want to do. But when you get up in the morning you check your e-mail and then you realize you're late for work so you scramble to get there on time, swearing you'll meditate when you get home. As you're about to clock out a friend texts you and asks if you want to drop by and see her new place so you do but you tell yourself that you really will meditate after that. Then you get home and you smell so you decide to shower. Then your dad calls and you haven't talked to him for a while so you catch up. Then you check your e-mail again. Then it's 10:00 p.m. and you have to get up early so you climb into bed, turn on the television, and realize you have made it so you just don't have time for that ten minutes of meditation that day. You wake up the next morning having sworn not to make the same mistake twice, but you repeat the same cycle. That is a prime example of speedy-busyness.

Frankly, you do have those ten minutes for meditation. We all do. It's just that you have spent an entire day convincing yourself that you don't, making everything other than your meditation practice a priority. It would, in fact, be less time-consuming to sit down and do your practice than exert all that mental energy convincing yourself that you can't do it. That is speedy-busyness, a form of avoiding your practice through conceptual means. It can be exhausting.

Speedy-busyness is one of the reasons I recommend that people establish consistency early on in their meditation practice. If you have a set place you go to meditate, that serves as the extra impetous to galvanize you to sit down and practice, and you're not convincing yourself that you don't have the time to set up your practice space. Alternatively, if you say, "I meditate after my morning coffee every day, Monday to Friday," then you will build out your schedule to include your meditation practice. It will not keep falling to the back burner like it would if you just say, "I meditate in the morning." If you consistently meditate for ten minutes and pace yourself to do it daily for a period of time, then it starts to become a new habit that you build into your life alongside your other habits, such as showering or getting dressed. Getting specific with these commitments is important in overcoming speedy-busyness. Consistency is one of the best antidotes to this difficult obstacle.

DISHEARTENMENT

Disheartenment is considered the third obstacle to meditation. Because meditation is such a gradual path, where it may take weeks or months before you start to notice you become more present or calmer, people often get disheartened. They think that meditation isn't working properly, or they aren't doing it right, because they are not immediately at peace with themselves after a week of consistent practice. Once again, this is a normal thing to wonder about. But the effects of meditation are subtle and it does take time to manifest off the cushion, so in the meantime we must work to overcome this obstacle.

The main antidote to the obstacle of disheartenment is based in the very first thing we talked about at the beginning of this book: we need to have a strong intention for our practice. At first our intention may be that we don't want to carry so much stress in our body all the time or we want to learn to work with our emotions in a healthy way. Whatever it is, that simple reminder of "why" is going to get us off our butts and onto the meditation seat when we feel disheartened.

This antidote is a bit like the pep talk a coach gives in any sports movie. You're in the locker room at halftime, down and out because the rival team, Disheartenment, is kicking your butt. The coach (which is in reality you staring at yourself in the mirror) looks you in the eye and says, "Kid. You know why you're in this game. Hold to that reason. Say it out loud. Keep it in your heart. Now go back on that field and give it all you got." Remembering why you're in the game to begin with fuels you when you feel disheartened.

If you want, you can even check in with yourself in front of the mirror when you feel disheartened. For me it doesn't have to be looking at myself in the mirror. As I sit down to meditate I can simply state out loud why I do it or write my reason down and it has the same effect. I remember what's important, my motivation for doing this work, and that overcomes any feeling of disheartenment that may arise.

In my case, I have found that over the years meditation has made me a better, more present person. The line between being present with the breath and being present with friends and family has dissolved a fair amount; it has become the instrument through which I am able to be in my body and in my world.

If you somehow glossed over the first chapter I encourage you to contemplate this "Why do I meditate?" question. If you have been meditating for a while it might be helpful to check in with yourself at this point and ask it anew. Perhaps initially you wanted to start a practice to be less stressed out but gradually your perspective has shifted and you see that meditation is having a positive effect on your life. Your motivation might shift as well, and now you think, "I want to be more present with others, knowing that this is when I am happiest" or "I want to be able to be of benefit to the world as a result of this practice."

When you are down in the dumps about how hard meditation practice is, it is this simple step of reminding yourself of your personal "why" that will get you back onto the meditation seat and once more enjoying your practice. In some sense this is simply powering through the times when your meditation practice feels like a drag. There is no pill we can pop or mantra we can recite that will magically make meditation easy so we won't ever get disheartened again. We simply have to stick with the practice until disheartenment eases its hold over us and we once more recall why the meditation practice is essential to what we are cultivating in our lives.

The Zen master Suzuki Roshi was once asked, "What is nirvana?" He gave a very straightforward answer, which seems to address this particular obstacle as well. He said, "Seeing one thing through to the end." When you feel disheartened, remember that becoming awake is not that difficult in the grand scheme of things. It is simply seeing one thing through to the end. In this case, that one thing is establishing and maintaining a meditation practice.

Laziness, speedy-busyness, and disheartenment will come up for us. As I said before, these are umbrella terms for a myriad of obstacles that might arise. It is not a bad thing that these obstacles arise: they are testing the mettle of our practice. If meditation was always beautiful and easy then that would be indicative of a mind that has already found peace.

I don't know about you but I believe that the fact that obstacles arise to my meditation practice are really just gentle reminders that I still have some ways to go in taming my own mind and the importance of doing so. These obstacles serve as signposts along the way of our spiritual journey, each one pointing the way toward becoming more familiar with our own mind. Becoming familiar with our own mind is the purpose of this practice, so in that sense these three obstacles are all part of what it takes to be a proficient meditator. Let's look now to another side of what can feel difficult during our meditation practice: working with emotions.

STEP 7 / WORK WITH YOUR EMOTIONS

The more we engage our meditation practice the more we begin to glimpse the various elements of our own minds. From a Buddhist point of view our mind is fundamentally open, clear, and neutral. At the same time, the mind also creates thoughts, fantasies, and emotions. We should not think that our moments of peace are the "good" meditation periods and the moments when we are lost in thought are "bad." They are all part of the energetic display of our mind. Whatever arises is perfect because that is what is going on in your mind that day.

When you sit down to meditate you will notice that there are a whole swarm of thoughts about your life and daily activity that will come up. It's a bit like stopping on a busy city sidewalk and just standing there. You didn't notice the speed of the city before but now that you are not taking part in it the speed feels overwhelming. The same felt sense of your experience may occur when you sit down to meditate at the end of a busy day. You are pausing in the midst of the storm, but it is all a part of your mind.

There are also times when you intend to meditate on the breath but as soon as you begin you get distracted by a fantasy. It could be planning an upcoming talk or report for work or thinking through a romantic evening with a love interest but before you know it full minutes have passed and you have not been meditating at all. These fantasies are also part of the energetic display of your mind.

When you sit your thoughts may be less distracting than full-out fantasies. You may have discursive thoughts, where one thought arises such as "I should exercise more," and then you immediately think about how you don't like to go to the gym, which leads to the friend of yours who has offered to serve as a personal trainer for you, to the fact that she's dating a guy you don't like, to the feeling of hopelessness that if she can't find a good guy what are your odds, and so on. Your mind is flickering around like a hummingbird near a pool of sugar water: excited but without focus. Still, it's just your mind. With all of these types of thoughts that arise, the basic technique of acknowledging them, labeling them "thinking," and coming back to the breath will ultimately prove their undoing. You will be able to come back to the breath, although it may take longer than you would hope.

Some thoughts may be even more subtle than those mentioned thus far: they may be about the meditation practice itself. You may be sitting there and thinking, "Am I doing this right?" Or, "My back hurts." Or, "Am I breathing normally?" These thoughts are subtle enough that they will likely arise and dissolve without you doing much of anything. You may not even need to label them "thinking" but see that they float away of their own accord. They are just passing across your mind without your having to do anything at all.

One of the hardest types of thoughts to work with on the meditation cushion falls under the large umbrella known as emotions. Emotions come in all shapes and sizes but at the end of the day they are all still thoughts, albeit thoughts with a lot of energy behind them. There are emotions we feel that make our body light, like new love, so that it feels we are breezing through life. There are emotions we feel that make us sink into ourselves, like heartbreak, so that it feels like we can barely get out of bed. Sometimes an emotion feels fluid and open, coming and going through our being, and other times we get hooked by a strong emotion and feel led around by it like a dog on a leash. With many of these emotions it is harder to just say "thinking" and come back to the breath.

The type of strong emotions that come up again and again on the meditation cushion are often the type that hook us, taking our mind on a wild ride away from resting in the present moment. These stuck emotions are known in Tibetan as *klesha*. Klesha can be directly translated as "afflictive emotions." These are the emotions that come up, either on the meditation cushion or in our day-to-day life, that make us feel energetically drained. It is like when you have a fight with your spouse and cannot stop replaying the discussion you had in your head: what you could have said differently, or what you will say to prove you are right. While the story line plays out in your head it is only fueling the underlying emotion of anger or unease. You keep yourself going in this spiral to the point where it feels like you are afflicting yourself with negativity. You are left drained and lethargic, no longer able to connect with, much less enjoy, your life.

In order to learn to not cause harm to yourself you need to learn to work with emotions, starting with when they arise on the meditation seat. The key way we work with emotions is quite simple: we stay with them, allowing them to pass through us like a cloud across the sky. We do not act out on them or suppress them but acknowledge them as potent thoughts that are ultimately ephemeral.

In terms of working with emotions in public, or when you are going about your day-to-day life, this means you do not leap in and act on whatever impulses arise to sate your emotional desires. For instance, when your spouse is angry at you and you feel anger in response, refrain from acting out and going down your habitual road with that person.

For another example, imagine you are going through town and see a new jacket that you want. You feel the desire arise in you, and you want to follow the impulse to purchase that jacket. You must have it now. But you realize that you cannot afford it. Should you give in to your emotional impulse, which will mean you will be left broke and, while well dressed, you will feel a bit bad about yourself the next time you want to spend money on something more personally meaningful to you? Giving in to your emotional impulse will lead to unskillful behavior and your causing yourself harm. So the best thing to do is to not act on it but instead refrain from engaging the impulse that goes along with the emotion you are feeling. Although there are certainly worse tormenting emotions than the struggle to avoid impulse buying, that is just one example of how, on any given day, we might get hooked by an emotion and regret it later. Better to catch yourself and not go the habitual road.

The basic discipline that arises out of our meditation practice is to catch ourselves when we get stuck. If you are stuck in a fantasy and become aware of it you say, "Ah ha! I ought to come back to the breath." You are cutting through the habitual impulse to indulge in that fantasy and instead are disciplined enough to remember the instructions on staying with your breathing. That discipline will, over time, manifest off the cushion when you notice you are hooked by emotions in the rest of your life. Instead of indulging those, you walk away from the situation or don't respond in a habitual way. This is renunciation.

In this usage of *renunciation* we are not beating away the emotion or suppressing it. As the Tibetan Buddhist teacher Chögyam Trungpa Rinpoche has said, "Renunciation here means overcoming that very hard, tough, aggressive mentality that wards off any gentleness that might come into our heart."[1] You do not leap to the extreme judgmental attitude of "You jerk. Don't feel that way," and run from the potent experience. Nor do you push it down and pretend it doesn't exist. You apply the discipline of your meditation practice and simply rest with what is, even if it is a difficult emotional experience.

This day-to-day way of working with emotions is rooted in the inner practice of working with them on the meditation cushion. Day by day, practice session by practice session, we learn to work with the energy of an emotion as a transformative experience. We are getting to know our emotional well-being and seeing that whatever arises, be it an emotion considered conventionally "good," like love, or "bad," like heartbreak, it is just a reflection of our own mind.

You are learning that you don't need to jump off the meditation seat and go talk to that person you are heartbroken over or in love with and you don't need to squash that heartbreak or love because it's scary; you can just hold your seat. You can just remain with it, as you stay focused on the breath. Rest with whatever emotions arise. That is your practice.

I often talk to people who say this is fine and good but their partner just dumped them and they simply can't stay with that emotion of heartbreak. It's too much. I have found (and found it in my own experience) that we often don't mean we can't stay with heartbreak. What we mean is that we get caught up in the story lines around that emotion. When you sit down to meditate your mind doesn't immediately go to "Oh! My heart!" Or if it does that's only for a moment. It's so tender that it's hard to stay with that. So our mind churns up the most amazingly distracting thing it can come up with: here's why this happened. "I thought things were going well but clearly he has unresolved issues with his ex." "She cares too much about her career; she was never going to settle down and have a family." Whatever possibilities you can come up with, that's how the afflictive emotion hooks you and takes you for a ride around town—through the story line that accompanies the emotion.

My advice for anyone in this situation, or anyone working with a similarly visceral emotion, is to drop that story line. Over and over again. Underneath the story line is the raw emotion that needs to be looked at. The more you can stay with that emotion the less afflictive it becomes. It softens and becomes that much more ephemeral the more you are able to rest with it. In essence, you are sinking into your own body and learning to be with what is, not what could be. Instead of "Why did he or she leave me?" it can become "Where am I stuck?" or "Is this emotion moving or fixed?" "Is it big or small?" Through becoming inquisitive with the emotional experience we are undercutting its power over us. We are practicing gom, becoming familiar with ourselves in a deep and formidable way.

The practice of working with our emotions shows us that they are not obstacles or something to avoid or suppress; they are the method for us connecting more deeply to our body and our mind. We are learning to stay with emotions with gentleness and inquisitiveness. We do not need to become judgmental and think that emotions hinder our practice; through becoming curious about them and dropping the story line around them we learn more about ourselves and taste the wisdom that lies underneath that layer of concept.

It is gentleness that allows us to not reject our present experience. It is the ability to be mindful and aware that keeps us from wandering the endless hallways of past and future. It is inquisitiveness that keeps us fresh and curious about whatever arises in the here and now. We can then stay present and learn from whatever emotion has arisen. We can let it be our guide, moving us closer to the core of what we are, which is awake. Along those lines, let's explore that part of ourselves, our nature of peaceful abiding.

STEP 8 / DISCOVER PEACE

Having begun to meditate regularly, applying gentleness to your experience of working with obstacles and emotions, you may have had moments when your practice felt peaceful. You have been spending your time learning to ride the natural ebb and flow of the breath, relaxing fully into your body in the process. As a result a moment may have occurred where it occurred to you, "This is different." In that moment you may have discovered that underneath the torrential whirlwind of thoughts and emotions is what is referred to as your peaceful abiding nature.

I originally thought to make mention of this peaceful abiding core at the beginning of this book. However, it is better to have an experience of this state rather than a theoretical notion of what it is. I am hoping that at this point you may have an embodied sense of what I am referring to, as opposed to thinking that we are discussing philosophy. If you have not yet had a moment when you felt at peace during your practice then please trust me, it will come.

This peaceful abiding state is inherently what you are. It is the core of who you are. And it's not just you that has it, it's everyone. We all possess this innate wakefulness. This peaceful state is referred to as *tathagatha-garbha* in Sanskrit, which can be translated as "buddha nature." It is the notion that, just like the Buddha, you have the seed to wake up to your life and your world in a vast and profound way. You share the same potential that he had because your being is naturally peaceful.

At times you may doubt that statement, which is completely understandable. We spend so much of our time doubting that we can be peaceful. More often than not we think our basic nature is confused, aggressive, and messed up. That's the zone where most of our mental energy is spent, right? I remember early on in my meditation training a teacher pointed out that this peaceful state is akin to the sun shining in the sky. It is always there, brilliant and radiant. However, it is often obscured by clouds. These clouds come and go, just as our vitriolic thoughts and emotions do, and at times are so spread out that the sun is able to show its radiance.

The sun is our basic state, our wakefulness. Even though it is often dulled by transient obscurations that does not mean it is not shining bright and always available.

Another way to consider this innate state of awakeness is that we are basically good. Basic goodness is a term that is often used in the Shambhala Buddhist tradition. It denotes that the more familiar we are with our wakefulness the more we realize that we are basically kind, strong, and wise. In some religious traditions there is a belief that you are originally bad, or basically sinful. This is a one-hundred-and-eighty-degree turn away from that. At our core we are awake and good. That is our birthright. That is who we are.

As I began my own meditation practice, I didn't realize that this was an important point. I thought that the practice we are exploring was a calming thing to do, and if it allowed me to be more present in my day-to-day life that would be helpful as well. However, over time I have discovered that the entire path is just discovering your innate wakefulness and acting from it. That's it. There is nothing more you have to do. If you take one thing away from this book I hope it is this notion that you are already good and awake, you just have to discover this peace for yourself.

At this point I imagine you're ready to move on. "Peace. Great. Got it." But I feel the need to belabor this point because society has whispered in your ear from the time you were a child telling you the antithesis of what I'm trying to emphasize. From the billboards to the magazines to the societal expectations around education and careers you have continuously been told that you are not good enough. You are not worthy of much. You need fixing.

For many of us we are presented with a magic fix. In response to the poverty mentality that is embedded in us from society, we hear messages about how to get "better." Particularly in advertising culture, we are offered the idea that if you buy this new makeup or iPad or childcare product that all your problems will be solved. In other words, we have been conditioned to seek goodness, wholeness, outside of ourselves. We have been told that we need external circumstances, be it a new job, item we can buy, or even romantic partner, and then we will be truly happy.

I'm sad to break the news that this is not the case. The new job will lead to just as much stress if not more than the old one or you will work too many hours or not be as valued as you would have hoped. Whatever item you buy will break, you will get bored of it, or a new version will come out in six months and put yours to shame. Spending time with your romantic partner may be enjoyable but ultimately you will part ways: either in a breakup or in death. Both can be traumatic. So if you think you can seek everlasting happiness in external circumstances you are bound to be disappointed.

That was the bad news—that getting some new job or buying something new or dating someone new won't bring you everlasting happiness. I also have good news. I will let Chögyam Trungpa Rinpoche break it to you, as I think he put it best in one of his books: "Here is the really good news: We are intrinsically buddha, or intrinsically awake, and we are intrinsically good."[1] If we could actually believe that or, better yet, experience that, then we would be in good shape. Happiness is not unattainable; it is based in being with your existent experience, which means being with your innate wakefulness. In this very moment you can find contentment. In this instant you can enjoy yourself. That is because you are basically good.

I am not just venturing into the realm of Buddhist philosophy. I am saying that this notion of basic goodness, or innate wakefulness, can and will be experienced through meditation practice. Basic goodness can be experienced more fully when we slow down to the point where we experience natural peace. Through the tool of meditation we are essentially stepping up to the sky and parting the clouds, not allowing them to linger across the sun. We come back to the present moment, again and again, which is like blowing the clouds away. Thus we reveal what is underneath: the radiant sun, our peaceful abiding state.

In this sense meditation is a very practical route to the conclusion that we don't need to fix or improve anything. We are already good—we just need to discover that truth. Chögyam Trungpa, in the same book, entitled *The Heart of the Buddha,* went on to say, "The important point for us is to realize that we are basically good. Our only problem is that sometimes we don't actually acknowledge that goodness."[2] We don't need to run out and purchase basic goodness or peace. We discover it within ourselves, within the present moment. All we have to do is acknowledge that experience.

Once you have acknowledged this peaceful state it becomes easier to meditate. Before you might have said, "I bet this meditation thing will help calm me down." Now you say, "I have had an experience of being with what is. I have glimpsed this peaceful state. And I want to do that again." You have transitioned from an aspirational attitude to an experiential one. Now when you are feeling disheartened you don't have to generate a lot of mental activity to motivate yourself to go sit on the meditation cushion. You can just reflect on your experience and acknowledge that you want to continue to cultivate that way of being.

Experiencing one moment of peace during your meditation practice is more motivation to continue on this path than I could ever offer you in this book. I offer you words, and you can choose to trust them or not. When you have an experience of peace, that is something you can have true conviction in. That conviction is what is referred to as faith in the Buddhist tradition. You are not having faith in another person's ability to communicate their experience. You have faith in yourself. You have faith in your own experience of peace. To deepen that faith will take you very far in terms of continuing to meditate after you put down this book.

The beauty about the meditation practice, and something we will discuss in the conclusive chapters of this book, is that it will often manifest in your life off the meditation seat. As you go about your day and notice that you are being very present with a meal you might think, "Huh. This is a good meal but it is also a moment of peace." That is a moment where you revealed your basic nature, where you were able to relax to the point of exposing your brilliant, radiant being. And those are also moments when you develop further faith in your own experience about how meditation is helping you progress on your spiritual journey. They do not happen solely on the meditation cushion; they will happen throughout your life.

When you learn to connect, over and over again, with your basic goodness you also begin to acknowledge this goodness in others. You start to see how others have the same potential to be as present and peaceful as you do. There is one more piece of good news I want to offer at this point: since everyone is inherently awake, everything is workable. If I had to boil the spiritual path of working with others down to one concept it would be that if we can have conviction in our own goodness and that of others then we always have the potential to connect with them in a genuine and respectful manner.

One word my teacher Sakyong Mipham Rinpoche has been using a fair amount in this context is "worthy." If you are basically good that means there is nothing inherently wrong with you. So you are worthy of anything and everything. The same can be said for our lover, our boss, and that neighbor we just can't stand because they always play their music so loud. They possess the same peaceful abiding core. They may not always act from that radiant place. They may gather the clouds of confusion to themselves regularly, acting out in harmful ways. But they still have the same potential to wake up to their own goodness.

If you can have faith in your own goodness then you will more readily be available to see it in others. In that way you meet others not on the wavelength of "You're an obstacle to my happiness" but "I am worthy. You are worthy. There is potential for us to connect." By acknowledging the goodness in yourself and others you present an open, spacious platform for genuine interaction to take place.

It is up to you how you want to view the world. You could ignore those moments of peace and buy into society's point of view that you are basically messed up and need fixing. You could continue to take refuge in external circumstances, ranging from new advances to make in your career to new products to buy to new people to date, and see how that works out for you. Or you can rejoice in those moments of peace and through discovering your innate state make a conscious decision to cultivate conviction in that experience. You can learn to appreciate your life and your world through having faith in this discovery of your peaceful abiding state.

STEP 9 / BECOME A DHARMIC PERSON

Congratulations. You have the basics. You know how to meditate, you know why you meditate, and you're likely starting to see that it's not just about sitting on a meditation cushion; it's about training to be more present and awake in your daily life. At this juncture I want to switch into emphasizing just that: how to be a more awake person when you get off the meditation cushion.

A big part about getting a meditation practice started is how you manifest the qualities you have been cultivating when you get up. In other words, it is easy to study the *dharma*, or teachings laid out by the Buddha, but it is another thing entirely to embody them. Through meditating regularly you may have seen some subtle change in your life. You were more present when your date was telling you about herself the other night, or you're kinder to your mom. And maybe that's because you've been meditating. In that sense, you are already becoming a dharmic person, someone who embodies this meditation practice.

Becoming a dharmic person does not mean you put on airs and try to present yourself in ways that you are not. Just because you have been meditating does not mean you're enlightened or that you're some guru sent to save everyone else from their confused minds. It means you're working with yourself and—here's the important thing—becoming more yourself. The idea of becoming a dharmic person is exactly that: it is the process of becoming more comfortable with and aware of who you are and your innate capacity to be awake. That is what it means to embody the teachings.

In 1979 Chögyam Trungpa Rinpoche gave a talk where he elucidated what it means to be a dharmic person. He referred back to a very traditional set of teachings that come from the Kagyu lineage of Tibetan Buddhism. This is a very old lineage and I have found the teachings and examples of members of that lineage to be quite profound. In this case, Trungpa Rinpoche translated a list of qualities that a dharmic person embodies, thus laying out a handy road map for us to follow in striving to become that type of person. Without further ado, what follows are the seven qualities of a dharmic person as taught by Trungpa Rinpoche.

PASSIONLESSNESS

I have to admit that right off the bat the term *passionlessness* may cause confusion. The dharmic person experiences passionlessness, which does not mean that they are not passionate about helping others, bettering themselves, saving the world, and so on. It actually means that a dharmic person does not run from emotionally confusing situations.

Trungpa Rinpoche introduced this term and went on to talk about boredom. We are always trying to avoid boredom, right? When you come home you might turn on music or the TV just to be distracted as you settle in. That transition time is killer. Or when you are waiting for a bus or train you whip out your smartphone, that handy device that can thwart boredom with any number of factors: games, the Internet, texts from friends, and more. Through technology and other means most of us have gotten very good at avoiding boredom.

Long before the smartphone Trungpa Rinpoche pointed out this tendency to want to solve what he called "our boredom problem." He introduced *passionlessness* as a term to point out that we can experience boredom and other emotions without wallowing in them or getting hooked by them. We can just be there, with whatever arises. You don't have to leap in and try to do something whenever you are uncomfortable. When you are in a difficult situation, for example, you don't have to try to make everything perfect. You can just relax with your discomfort. That ability to be with emotional issues is being passionless, which is one quality of being a dharmic person.

CONTENTMENT

The second quality you can cultivate in the interest of being a dharmic person is contentment. In short, this quality is about being okay with who you are. It is having endless faith in your own goodness, which leads to your realizing that, you know what, you're okay. It builds on the previous quality in that you realize you don't need to fix or do anything. Contentment resides in this very moment.

Trungpa Rinpoche elaborated on this idea by saying that you don't have to expand upon yourself. You don't need to change anything about who you are. You can relax into being you. That's what being a dharmic person truly means. When obstacles arise, and they always do, you don't have to freak out and make everything okay again. You can lean into a situation without judgment of what "needs" to happen and just be present with what is happening, responding with what is most skillful. Trungpa Rinpoche commented on this sort of scenario when he said, "You can have some appreciation of obstacles becoming simplicity."[1] In other words, if you face obstacles with this sense of openness, things become simple. We don't need to complicate them with what we think needs to happen or ought to happen. We can approach them with a sense of appreciation of what they are and see them as part of our path.

PREVENTING TOO MANY ACTIVITIES

The third quality of being a dharmic person is very interesting: it's the idea that we don't need to churn up a lot of things for us to do. We can simplify our lives through our body, speech, and mind.

To break this down further we can be discerning about our body and the activity we engage in: Is it necessary? Good? Helpful? Timely? If not, then we probably don't need to engage it. That means that if you have certain habitual things you do that drain you of energy you ought to just cut those out. If you have a tendency to drink to excess and that means you lose full or half days to hangovers then maybe you ought to cut down on your drinking. Or if you have an online eBay addiction and you are continuously overdrawing your bank account maybe you should spend less time on that site. While simple enough to say, it's actually quite hard for us to break with negative habitual patterns. It takes time and energy for us to cut through the negative activity we engage in. When Trungpa Rinpoche says we should prevent too many activities he's pointing to this idea of simplifying our lives through being discerning with our actions.

Trungpa Rinpoche went on to discuss the speech element of preventing too many activities, which includes cutting down on nonfunctional talking. I have spent some of the best times of my life in silent meditation retreats and I have to say, shutting up for days to weeks is an eye-opening experience. You realize how much you talk without any sense of functionality. More often than not we see someone and verbally vomit all of our emotional garbage onto them, thus draining them of energy and leaving us feeling perhaps with a cathartic experience but not so uplifted either.

We can prevent too much activity with our speech. That means choosing our words carefully, and engaging subjects that matter to us. If you're out with a friend and you want to catch up with them then by all means communicate. But communicate what matters, as opposed to gossip, slander of others, lies, or harmful speech. Say what you mean, without adding in the unfiltered nonsense that most of us offer up as a means of connection.

The mind element of preventing too much activity is cutting down on mental entertainment. As you have likely experienced on the meditation cushion, more often than not your mind flits around like that hummingbird I mentioned earlier. We think of all the things we need. "Do I need an iPad for work? Or maybe I need to get laid to relax. Or perhaps some new shoes would make my life easier." The mind goes back and forth pursuing happiness endlessly.

In today's world there is always something new to do. We have the Internet and with it infinite possibilities of what we could be doing instead of what we're doing now. As a result we get lost in all the things we can do, say, and think and don't do anything properly, giving it our undivided attention. The dharmic person sees past that and reduces her or his activity so as to make space for the things that matter.

Good Conduct

I sort of feel like the fourth quality of a dharmic person should go without saying, but if you wish to embody the teachings of the Buddha you need to engage in good conduct. I realize that when I use this term "good conduct" I could end up writing a list of dos and don'ts as to what one should or should not do to be a dharmic person. That's not the point. If the point of this meditation practice is to be yourself, then it is up to you to determine what good conduct might look like.

The umbrella for good conduct, as Trungpa Rinpoche went on to point out, is that you have to be willing to work on yourself and also be of benefit to others. Those are the two main factors; what the specifics look like I leave up to you. Both working on yourself and working for others take time to sort out so don't feel like you have to be completely together before you begin to engage in good conduct. Similarly, if you intend to help others and sometimes make a mistake along the way it's not the end of the world. You learn from those situations and strive to not repeat your mistakes. Over time you get better and better at being of benefit to others. The point here is to see whatever you are doing as an extension of your meditation practice in regard to cultivating mindfulness and awareness. If you can do that you will continue to succeed at bettering yourself and others simultaneously.

Awareness of the Teacher

The fifth quality of a dharmic person is having an awareness of a teacher. For advanced Buddhist practitioners who might have one teacher they work with regularly, this part of the very traditional Kagyu list means that you should always have that individual on your mind in some shape or form. For newer meditation practitioners this means that you should have some relationship with a teacher or with realized people (or both) who inspire you to continue to engage in the other qualities of a dharmic person.

This is actually an important point that I don't want to gloss over. For someone who is trying to establish a meditation practice, books and sitting alone at home are great. But it's helpful to have a community supporting that endeavor. So explore local meditation and Buddhist communities in your area. If you don't know how to do that the Internet can help or you can reach out to me. The beauty of being a meditator in America today is that within one city there are a gazillion good communities of meditators doing what you want to do. So go hang out with them and feel that level of support.

In addition, if you connect with a teacher or meditation instructor at that place, try and form a relationship with them. You don't need to worship them or put them on a pedestal, but if you find someone at one of these Buddhist centers who is behaving in the way you ought to behave, try to spend time with that person. They may inspire you as well.

Prajna is a Sanskrit term that can be translated as "superior knowing." It is the act of seeing things for what they are. It is when you step out of thinking solely about what would make you happy, or the way you think things should be, and just be with what is. It is also the idea that you should understand who you are.

To that end, you can take pride in deepening your understanding of these teachings. You can use the dharma to further explore yourself and your world. Prajna is not just about sitting on the cushion and seeing what's up with your mind that day. It is relating to postmeditation situations, such as conversations or meals, as opportunities to be a dharmic person. Each of these scenarios is a chance for you to further see things for what they are. Each of these times are moments when you can drop your judgmental mind at the door, stop thinking solely about yourself, and just lean into what is actually going on. When you do that you are not taking time off from anything; your life is infused with the dharma.

Attitude of Goodness

The final quality of a dharmic person is that your very being is infused with an attitude of goodness.

Once again, it's not like you have magically transformed into a better being because you started meditating. You're just more you. You're a you that is aware of both the sanity and insanity that rages inside your mind and is able to accommodate both with equanimity.

The more familiar you are with yourself the more comfortable you will be in manifesting your own goodness. Through both your meditation practice and your postmeditation contemplations you have experienced this goodness. It's one thing for you to know that you're basically good. It's another thing to share your experience of that. This is not to say that you should go out and proselytize to others about how you've found meditation and how they will be better for following in your footsteps. This is subtly expressing your own confidence in who you are, through just being a kind, decent human being.

In some sense, all seven of these qualities of being a dharmic person could be summarized by that term: just be a kind, decent human being as a result of the fact that you are more mindful and aware than you might have been if you were not meditating. If you are able to do that then the teachings of the Buddha—the dharma—are no longer something that is way out there and separate from you and your life. They are a part of your being. When you feel that you view the world through the lens of meditation, exhibiting these basic qualities, then you know you are a dharmic person. You have allowed the meditation practice to change you, not into a different person, but into realizing more of who you already are.

STEP 10 / RELAX

As we come to the end of our time together I want to say that I think we've covered just about everything you need to get a meditation practice off the ground. I hope you have a sense as to your personal intention for why you're meditating. In addition, you have the actual technique that you can do on a daily basis. You have an understanding of mindfulness and awareness and how these innate aspects of yourself can aid your practice. You (hopefully) have established a consistent time, place, and amount of time you meditate each week.

You also have an understanding as to what will arise in meditation practice. You know that it's not easy and that you have to continue to remember to be gentle to yourself as you engage this path. Gentleness is an important foundational quality to cultivate as you learn to work with the primary obstacles that arise in your practice: laziness, speedy-busyness, and disheartenment. The more you practice consistently the more you see how your habitual mind with its myriad display of emotions works, and the more you discover your inherently peaceful state and can act from a point of goodness.

At that point you transition from the meditation cushion and this practice being something you do at home to something you embody in the rest of your life. You become a dharmic person, embodying the seven qualities outlined in the previous chapter so that you manifest your meditative mindset. You are now ready for the final, really difficult step in your journey to establish a meditation practice: you have to relax.

This step of relaxing is actually easier said than done. We are all so tightly wound. As I mentioned earlier, I live in New York City and I see many young people here who are ambitious. Many of those young ambitious people aspire to university degrees and they face a fiercely competitive environment. Once upon a time you would get good grades in high school and could get into a good college. Now my friends who are parents are trying to get their kids into the best kindergartens, knowing that leads to the best middle schools, then the best high schools, which culminates in a great college degree, which, frankly, in this economy doesn't mean a whole lot in terms of getting a great job. Yet instead of relaxing and seeing how ludicrous this system is, people are buying SAT prep cards for their toddlers. I can't help but think that no matter how tightly wound some of my peers may be today their children will be walking balls of stress tomorrow.

For most of us this idea of needing to "succeed" dominates our thinking. We believe we need to get the best job possible, and when we are promoted to a position we desire we are already looking toward another one with a higher salary. We have a nice time alone but wouldn't it be nice to have a really hot, fun, smart spouse who appreciates and gets us? Maybe we should try a million dating websites and bars to select *the* perfect person and then we will be successful romantically. We can get rich and use all of our money to buy nice things but yet those nice things seem to break down or we get bored with them. But owning them means we're successful, right? All of this may feel a bit hollow to you. It certainly does to me.

I am guessing that when you picked up this book you might have had the idea that it would help you be successful at meditating. The trick is, of course, that all you're being successful at is being more you. You're just learning to relax with who you already are, relax with whatever arises on the meditation cushion, and relax with both the pleasurable and painful elements of your life when you get off that meditation seat. That's what success means in a meditative context. In other words, let's not get uptight here. If you got into meditation to learn to relax, then make sure you're not using it as another thing to get wound up about.

One way to view this final step in your journey is that you should relinquish your attachment to struggle. It may sound like an odd thing to accuse you of, but I'm a firm believer that we all habitually make things harder on ourselves than we need to. In particular when you meditate it's easy to take this supremely simple practice and try to complicate it. I mean, all you need to do is be with the breath. How simple is that?

At any given time I meet with a handful of newer meditators regularly as they get their practice going. It's always surprising to me just how complicated they try to make this meditation practice. As they go from wondering if their eyes are doing what they should be doing to feeling like they have an abnormal breath to feeling like they are in danger of leaving their bodies if they meditate, I sit and listen to whatever is coming up. At the same time I recall what my teachers would tell me when I was a new meditator and tried to overthink my practice. They would say, "Keep sitting." That's it. I often try to be a bit more verbose and supportive with the people I meet with, and if I'm doing a good job they will look up at the end and say, "So it sounds like I just need to keep sitting." That's right. If you keep sitting you will relax out of this idea that meditation practice (and other elements of your life) should be a struggle. You can just relax. I swear.

I have a friend who is a ballet dancer. When I asked her about the incredible precision that takes place in any of her performances she told me about how it came down to learning what she had to do thoroughly and then, when it came time to perform, she had to relax. I was reminded of one Tibetan Buddhist teacher talking about how they had learned about race-car drivers: that they have to be very precise, but if they are uptight they will end up getting in an accident. Instead they just have to know what they are doing and relax, and then they drive well. In both of these scenarios the idea is to know what you are doing and then to relax while doing it. This advice can be applied to the many forms of relaxation I am recommending.

RELAX WITH WHATEVER ARISES ON THE MEDITATION CUSHION

The basis for learning to relax is the time you spend on the meditation seat. Yes, "keep sitting" is basically the best advice for anyone in their first year of meditation practice. However, in my experience the second-best piece of advice is to maintain a sense of humor and delight as you practice. This harks back to the discussion on gentleness, but we're adding in a sense of playfulness on top of that self-kindness. When you are fantasizing about having sex with that same person for the millionth time instead of coming back to the breath you could get frustrated with yourself or just realize how silly the whole thing is and laugh at it. Have a sense of humor about your crazy, hummingbird mind. If you can laugh at your mental display then you are experiencing relaxation at its finest.

Relax with Both the Pleasurable and Painful Elements of Your Life

Whether life hands you lemons or lemonade, relax with each situation and appreciate it. In other words, there will be times in life when things are awesome. You are content with your life: you have great friends and a supportive partner, you enjoy your work and feel like it helps people, and overall life feels fine. Enjoy that for what it is; don't feel like you need to "fix" anything. Relax with your experience of contentment.

There will be other times when life feels really

hard. A loved one dies. You lose your job and fear for your financial security. Your partner leaves you unexpectedly. You feel like the world has fallen apart and you want to stop meditating and instead freak out. First, don't stop meditating. If nothing else it will ground you in your emotional experience and you will become more familiar with it. Second, relax. Just as when everything was going super well, you don't need to "fix" anything. Relax with your experience of heartbreak or disappointment. Whatever arises we can relax with. That is the beauty of your meditation practice showing up in the rest of your life. Whatever comes up is a part of your path.

Relax with Who You Already Are

If I can impart one final piece of advice, it is to relax with who you are. In essence, this is the entire Buddhist path. If you can learn to relax both on the cushion and when you are traveling through the rest of your life then you will connect with all the various aspects of who you are. And each of those aspects, be they horrifying and insane or totally fun and sane, are just a part of your overall makeup. If you can see that, then you realize that you are already sacred. So why not relax with conviction in your own sacredness?

The path of meditation is a training in being.

When I ask that you relax with who you already are I am asking you to be you. You don't have to figure out what to be or what to do to exhibit more of yourself. You don't need to struggle to figure out how to be when you go out to a party or are at work. You can just be you. That is the point here. Meditation is just a tool to let you be you: to bring a sense that you are actually good enough, worthy enough, and kind, strong, and smart enough to handle whatever arises. That is your right. So embrace it.

I hope this meditation practice is helpful to you and transforms you as it has transformed me. I hope you become kinder and more authentic as a result of the practice. I hope you have moments when you realize just how good you are and those moments strengthen your ability to deal with whatever arises in life. I got into this writing gig because I thought if just one person picked up my first book and started meditating I would call that a success. I have confidence in this simple technique and the power its simplicity holds. Because if you are that person who starts meditating and is transformed by the practice then I know you will go on to do great things. This world needs people who are working to become more self-aware and kind. We need a hundred million of them. But let's start with you. Please join me in meditating regularly. I'm here for you and we can do this practice together.

NOTES

STEP 3. APPLY THE ULTIMATE TAG-TEAM COMBO

1. Sakyong Mipham Rinpoche, *The Shambhala Principle* (New York: Harmony, 2013), 124.
2. Pema Chödrön, *Comfortable with Uncertainty* (Boston: Shambhala Publications, 2008), 187.

STEP 4. BE CONSISTENT

1. Sakyong Mipham Rinpoche, *Ruling Your World: Ancient Strategies for Modern Life* (New York: Three Rivers Press, 2006), 24.

STEP 5. BE GENTLE

1. Sakyong Mipham Rinpoche, *The Shambhala Principle* (New York: Harmony, 2013), 52.

STEP 7. WORK WITH YOUR EMOTIONS

1. Chögyam Trungpa Rinpoche, *The Collected Works of Chögyam Trungpa*, vol. 8 (Boston: Shambhala Publications, 2004), 396.

STEP 8. DISCOVER PEACE

1. Chögyam Trungpa Rinpoche, *The Heart of the Buddha* (Boston: Shambhala Publications, 2010), 6.
2. Ibid, 193.

STEP 9. BECOME A DHARMIC PERSON

1. Chögyam Trungpa Rinpoche, *The Collected Works of Chögyam Trungpa*, vol. 2 (Boston: Shambhala Publications, 2004), 486.

RESOURCES

FURTHER READING

The Buddha Walks into a Bar by Lodro Rinzler. My first book.

Turning the Mind into an Ally by Sakyong Mipham Rinpoche. My recommended go-to read for the technique of meditation.

The Shambhala Principle by Sakyong Mipham Rinpoche. A beautiful manifesto on how to bring basic goodness into society.

Work, Sex, Money: Real Life on the Path of Mindfulness by Chögyam Trungpa Rinpoche. A lovely exposition on the intersection of everyday life and meditation.

Shambhala: The Sacred Path of the Warrior by Chögyam Trungpa Rinpoche. A foundational text on Shambhala Buddhism.

Ruling Your World by Sakyong Mipham Rinpoche. A great book overall, but a terrific exploration of the Six Ways of Ruling.

Only Don't Know by Zen Master Seung Sahn. Letters to and responses from a Zen master.

The 37 Practices of a Bodhisattva by Ngulchu Thogme. Each practice is worth spending at least a day contemplating.

Lovingkindness by Sharon Salzberg. Because the first step will always be offering love to yourself.

Comfortable with Uncertainty by Pema Chödrön. A compilation of teachings from Pema Chödrön, each chapter being short enough to read in a few minutes before bed.

Living Beautifully by Pema Chödrön. A terrific exposition on how to do just that.

The Wisdom of a Broken Heart by Susan Piver. An excellent read for anyone feeling heartbroken.

Awake at Work by Michael Carroll. Mr. Carroll has spent decades applying meditation principles to the workplace environment: a great read.

A Guide to the Bodhisattva's Way of Life (also known as *The Way of the Bodhisattva*) by Shantideva. A pivotal text on the Mahayana path.

One City: A Declaration of Interdependence by Ethan Nichtern. An exploration of interconnectivity.

WEBSITES

www.lodrorinzler.com. My personal website with written, audio, and video teachings. There are also links to the work I do in the realm of authentic leadership training.

www.shambhala.org. Teachings and resources for supporting your meditation practice, including a list of Shambhala centers that you can visit for in-person teachings.

www.samadhicushions.com. A great source for meditation cushions, malas, and other supplies.

www.reciprocityfoundation.org. Profits from meditation cushion sales go toward supporting homeless youth in New York City.

CONTACT INFO

E-mail: info@lodrorinzler.com
Twitter: @lodrorinzler
Facebook: Lodro Rinzler
Bat Signal: A giant *L* will suffice.

Believe what you've heard about meditation: it'll focus your mind, open your heart, and sometimes surprise you with insight. And it's not complicated to learn. In fact, everything you need to get started is contained in the pages of this little book. Lodro Rinzler begins by challenging you to ask yourself why you want to meditate in the first place (good news—there's no wrong answer!). With your intention thus in place, he teaches you all the basics, along with advice for making your meditation practice a priority no matter how busy you are. He then shows you how to bring the wisdom and compassion you discover in meditation into all other areas of your life.

LODRO RINZLER is a teacher in the Shambhala Buddhist lineage and founder of the Institute for Compassionate Leadership. He is also the author of *The Buddha Walks into a Bar...*, *The Buddha Walks into the Office*, and *Walk Like a Buddha: Even if Your Boss Sucks, Your Ex Is Torturing You, and You're Hungover Again*. For more of Lodro visit www.lodrorinzler.com.

Cover art: Shutterstock/banderlog
Cover design by Daniel Urban-Brown
©2014 Shambhala Publications, Inc.
Printed in U.S.A.
♻Printed on recycled paper

WWW.SHAMBHALA.COM

ISBN 978-1-61180-165-1

US $11.95   CAN $13.95

SHAMBHALA
Boston & London